Manipulation

RESOURCES FOR BIBLICAL LIVING

Bitterness: The Root That Pollutes
Deception: Letting Go of Lying
Discontentment: Why Am I So Unhappy?
Divorce: Before You Say "I Don't"
Fear: Breaking Its Grip
Grief: Learning to Live with Loss
In-Laws: Married with Parents
Judgments: Rash or Righteous
Manipulation: Knowing How to Respond
Motherhood: Hope for Discouraged Moms
Problems: Solving Them God's Way
Self-Image: How to Overcome Inferiority Judgments
Selfishness: From Loving Yourself to Loving Your Neighbor
Temptation: Applying Radical Amputation to Life's Sinful Patterns

Lou Priolo, series editor

Manipulation

Knowing How to Respond

LOU PRIOLO

P&R PUBLISHING

P.O. BOX 817 • PHILLIPSBURG • NEW JERSEY 08865-0817

The contents of this book have been adapted and expanded, with permission, from several of the author's previous books: primarily *The Heart of Anger* and *Getting a Grip* (both from Calvary Press).

Unless otherwise indicated, Scripture quotations are from the NEW AMERICAN STANDARD BIBLE®. Copyright © 1960, 1962, 1963, 1968, 1971, 1972, 1973, 1975, 1977, 1995 by The Lockman Foundation. Used by permission.

Italics within Scripture quotations indicate emphasis added.

Printed in the United States of America

Library of Congress Cataloging-in-Publication Data

Priolo, Lou.
 Manipulation : knowing how to respond / Lou Priolo.
    p. cm. — (Resources for biblical living)
 Includes bibliographical references.
 ISBN 978-1-59638-128-5 (pbk.)
 1. Control (Psychology)—Religious aspects—Christianity. 2. Manipulative behavior. 3. Interpersonal relations—Religious aspects—Christianity. I. Title.
 BV4597.53.C62P75 2008
 248.4—dc22
                        2008034187

SO, YOU THINK you are being manipulated! My guess is that the person you suspect of being manipulative is someone you love or respect. That's what makes it so difficult to know for sure. When you try to talk to this individual about your concerns, you end up thinking that *you* are the one who is at fault. Maybe you're just being too temperamental about the matter.

Perhaps you are. But by the time you're through with this little booklet, I pray you'll be able to figure things out. What's more, if in fact you are being manipulated, you should be well on your way to putting a stop to it. At the very least, you will learn how to remove the little handle on your back by which manipulators push you in one direction and pull you in the other.

What Is Manipulation?

Webster's dictionary defines the verb *manipulate* as "to control or play upon by artful, unfair, or insidious means."[1] For a Christian, manipulation is using unbiblical means of controlling or influencing others. More specifically, manipulation is often an attempt to gain control of another individual or situation by inciting an *emotional reaction* rather than a

---

1. There is an interesting biblical term that may come close to describing manipulative individuals. The word is *oppressor*. There are several Hebrew words that have been translated into English as *oppressor*. Take the word '*asoq*, for example. According to the *Theological Wordbook of the Old Testament* (R. L. Harris, G. L. Archer, B. K. Waltke [Chicago: Moody Press, 1999], 705), the word is concerned with acts of abuse of power or authority, the burdening, trampling, and crushing of those lower in station. Another interesting word for *oppressor* is *tok*. Used in Proverbs 29:13, the term connotes fraud and deceitfulness. As we will see in a moment, manipulators deceitfully conceal significant information from those whom they are trying to control.

biblical response from that individual. It often is accomplished through intimidation. This involves selfishly coercing someone *to* or inhibiting someone *from* a particular course of action by (directly or indirectly) causing him to sense some kind of threat.

Rather than trying to resist and overcome the temptation, our first thoughts when we are manipulated are normally to lick our wounds. George K. Simon in his book *In Sheep's Clothing* explains:

> All of us have weaknesses and insecurities that a clever manipulator might exploit. Sometimes, we're aware of these weaknesses and how someone might use them to take advantage of us. . . . Sometimes we're unaware of our biggest vulnerabilities. Manipulators often know us better than we know ourselves. They know what buttons to push, when and how hard. Our lack of self-knowledge sets us up to be exploited.[2]

In the tenth chapter of Luke, Martha "was distracted with all her preparations; and she came up to Him [Jesus] and said, 'Lord, *do You not care* that my sister has left me to do all the serving alone? Then tell her to help me' " (v. 40).

Martha wanted assistance with her food preparations and was frustrated (angry) that her sister left her to do all the serving by herself. Rather than telling the Lord exactly what she wanted (help with the cooking), she first attempted to play on His emotions (sympathy and perhaps guilt). "Do You not care?" Another element of manipulation can be seen in Martha's response. Here she was attempting to motivate someone to fulfill her personal desires without clearly stating them. An appeal for sympathy, rightly expressed, is not necessarily wrong. But for such an appeal to be seen as sincere, the true

2. George K. Simon Jr., *In Sheep's Clothing: Understanding and Dealing with Manipulative People* (Little Rock, AR: A. J. Christopher & Co., 1996), 79.

desire behind such a request should normally be expressed also (in this case, Martha's desire for help). To do otherwise is usually dishonest because it is concealing necessary information from the person to whom the appeal is made.

Before looking at how Jesus responded to this and other manipulative ploys by friends and foes alike, let's take a closer look at the concept of emotional manipulation. The table on page nine will serve to simplify and illustrate the ways and means of manipulation. As we continue, try to put yourself in the seat of a manipulator. Perhaps you have never tried to see things through "manipulative eyes," but doing so just might help you better understand what may be going on behind the scenes of controlling behaviors.[3]

The first column, "Manipulator's Behavior," lists some of the more common ways manipulators tend to manipulate their victims. When dealing with manipulative people, it is important to remember that the manipulator may or may not be consciously aware that he is being manipulative. From a very young age (even before he could pronounce the word *manipulation*, let alone know what it was), the manipulator may have trained himself to get what he wanted by being manipulative. All he may have understood at the time was that by doing or saying certain things he could get what he wanted. So he practiced and practiced his manipulative behaviors, perhaps not even knowing until later (if he ever realized at all) that he had become manipulative.

The second column, "Desired Emotional Response from the Victim," pinpoints what the manipulator may want his

3. We cannot know for sure what is going on in the heart of another without his *first* disclosing it to us. Indeed, the Bible forbids us from making such judgments about the thoughts and motives of others (see 1 Cor. 5:4). The purpose of reviewing this material is not for you to attempt to "read the minds" of your potential manipulators, but rather to help you understand what is really at the heart of much manipulative behavior. Should you have the opportunity to minister to those who attempt to manipulate you *and* can get them to reveal their thoughts and motives to you, you may be able to use this material to help them identify and correct the sinful activities of their own hearts.

manipulative behavior to produce in the heart of his victim. Again, he may have practiced his manipulative ways for so long that at any given moment he may not even be aware of what his desires really are. (On the other hand, as we will see, many manipulators are very well aware of what they are doing and pursue their selfish desires with a vengeance!)

The third column, "What the Manipulator Really Wants to Accomplish," identifies the selfish purpose of the manipulator's ploy.

The fourth column, "What Idolatrous Desire Rules in the Manipulator's Heart," suggests possible motives for the manipulation. That is, it specifies those potential chief desires (those things that he inordinately loves) that may be so intense that the manipulator is willing to resort to sinful behavior in order to obtain what he loves and longs for.

Chances are good that there is something your manipulator is wanting badly enough to fight for. He resorts to sinful (deceptive, underhanded) methods of fighting and warring to get what he desires. Remember that manipulators often portray themselves as "helpless," "hurting," "frightened," or "wounded" when the truth is that they are hostile, aggressive warriors (fighters).

> Where do wars and fights come from among you? Do they not come from your desires for pleasure that war in your members? You lust and do not have. You murder and covet and cannot obtain. You fight and war. Yet you do not have because you do not ask. You ask and do not receive, because you ask amiss, that you may spend it on your pleasures. (James 4:1–3 NKJV)

When people knowingly resort to manipulation in order to get something, it's because the *something* they want is wrong. Now, it's not because that something is necessarily sinful *in and of itself*, but because they want that something (as good as it might be) too much. The fact that a Christian is willing to sin by manipulating someone in order to acquire what he longs for is evidence that he has made an idol of it. An idolatrous desire is anything we want so much that we are willing to sin in order to have it.

Table 1: Elements of Manipulative Behavior

Manipulator's Behavior	Possible Desired Emotional Response from the Victim	What the Manipulator May Really Want to Accomplish	What Idolatrous Desire May Rule in the Manipulator's Heart
Accusations	Guilt	To procrastinate	Love of pleasure
Criticisms	Shame	To avoid obligations	Love of power (control)
Crying	Embarrassment	To change his victim's mind	Love of praise
"Why" questions	Hurt	To procrastinate	Love of money
Obligatory statements	Anger	To impose unbiblical standards	Love of whatever
Sulking / pouting	Fear / anxiety / intimidation	To influence or control decisions	
Withholding affection		To gain or maintain the upper hand	
Giving the cold shoulder		To get what he wants	
Physical abuse			
Flattery and cajolery			
Planting seeds of anxiety			
Playing the victim			

A Biblical Response to Foolishness

We are ready to take a look at Christ's approach to manipulative people. Jesus never answered a foolish individual with a foolish response. He never fought folly with folly. In communicating with fools, He never employed communication forms that violated Scripture. Although He did respond to foolishness, He did not respond in kind. In other words, He did not allow the fool with whom He was talking to drag Him down to his level by playing the same sinful communication games as His opponent. Neither did He allow the fool to walk away from the conversation believing that he was wise in his own eyes.

What He did do when responding to foolish verbiage was to show the fool his own folly. Those who approached Christ with the intent to manipulate Him (often by trying to make Him look foolish) walked away realizing how foolish they themselves were. Of course, this thwarted their schemes, which resulted in some of them becoming rather frustrated (angry at Him).

Time will not permit the development of all the appropriate biblical responses to a fool. There is one reply, however, that we must consider, since out of this biblical injunction flows the essence of Christ's adeptness at dealing with manipulators. He consistently employed the wisdom of Proverbs 26:4–5 in dealing with foolish requests, setups, and attempts to control Him. Proverbs 26:4 says, "Do not answer a fool according to his folly, or you will also be like him." And Proverbs 26:5 tells us to "answer a fool as his folly deserves, that he not be wise in his own eyes."

The following chart contrasts the difference between answering a fool according to his folly and answering a fool as his folly deserves.

Table 2: Answering a Foolish Person

According to his folly (Prov. 26:4)	As his folly deserves (Prov. 26:5)
1. The manipulatee is drawn into a conflict by the manipulator.	1. The manipulatee quickly gains control of the conversation.
2. The manipulator is allowed to effectively employ sinful manipulative behaviors against the manipulatee.	2. The manipulator is confronted biblically by the manipulatee when manipulative behaviors are employed.
3. The manipulatee reacts with a snappy comeback motivated by emotions other than concern for the manipulator.	3. The manipulatee responds out of love with a well-thought-out biblical answer that aims at exposing the manipulator's folly.
4. The manipulatee resorts to defending himself, justifying his actions, blame-shifting, answering "why" questions, arguing, etc.	4. The manipulatee identifies and effectively puts an end to the manipulative behavior of the manipulator.
5. The manipulatee walks away feeling guilty, intimidated, frustrated, exasperated, like a failure or victim.	5. The manipulatee walks away confident that he, by God's grace, has silenced the manipulator's folly.
6. The manipulator walks away with the satisfaction of knowing that he has punished or manipulated his victim.	6. The manipulator walks away unsuccessful at his attempted manipulation, and quite possibly realizing that he has played the fool.

Scripture records numerous examples of individuals who attempted to manipulate Christ. Of course, not one person ever succeeded! Christ's responses to those manipulative individuals typically involved two effective techniques. These two responses are frequently found together, but almost always at least one of them was employed.

Before explaining what they are, I must first give a warning. Christ could not sin. His motives, therefore, for responding to the foolish requests and questions of those who wanted to manipulate Him were impeccable. He always wanted to please and glorify His Father. For you to attempt to use the biblical resources that you are about to learn for selfish ends is wrong. To do so not only would be evil (the very evil you are trying to deal with biblically—manipulation); it would not be blessed by God and would likely backfire. In other words, to use biblical weapons (which were meant for the purpose of fighting evil) in order to get what *you* want rather than what *God* wants is sinful—it would be nothing more than a gimmick to manipulate others, including God Himself. If you expect God to bless you in your efforts to keep others from manipulating you, you must be certain that your motives are unselfish before you attempt to use these resources.

Now that you've been duly warned, I will unpack these two antimanipulation devices for you. First, Jesus appealed to (the conscience of) the manipulator to fulfill specific, personal, biblical responsibilities (which typically he had neglected to fulfill). Second, He appealed to God's Word (or at least to God's will as found in God's Word) as the standard by which the manipulator is to be judged.

Jesus Responds to Martha

For instance, getting back to the story of Mary and Martha found in the tenth chapter of Luke, how did Christ deal with Martha's attempt to pressure Him into giving her what she wanted?

> Now as they were traveling along, He entered a certain village; and a woman named Martha welcomed Him into her home. And she had a sister called Mary, who was seated at the Lord's feet, listening to His word. But Martha was distracted with all her preparations; and she came up to Him and said, "Lord, do You not care that my sister has left me to do all the serving alone? Then tell her to help me." But the Lord answered and said to her, "Martha, Martha, you are worried and bothered about so many things; but only one thing is necessary, for Mary has chosen the good part, which shall not be taken away from her." (Luke 10:38–42)

First, He made an appeal to her personal responsibilities. He said, "Martha, Martha, you are *worried* and *bothered* about so many things; but only one thing is necessary." Jesus said elsewhere that His disciples ought not to worry (Matt. 6:25) or be troubled (John 14:1). Therefore, Martha was not fulfilling at least two biblical responsibilities. Jesus reproved her. He then reminded her that her only necessary responsibility was to sit at His feet and hear the Word of God.

Second, He made a subtle yet definite appeal to God's will. He said, "Only one thing is *necessary*, for Mary has chosen the *good* part, which shall not be taken away from her." During His own temptation when Jesus was in the wilderness for forty days, He said, "Man shall not live on bread alone, but on every word that proceeds out of the mouth of God" (Matt. 4:4; Luke 4:4). Consequently, Mary, who was feasting on the Word of God, was commended for doing the good (right) thing. The fact that Jesus called what Mary had "chosen" to do "necessary" and "good" implies that she was doing God's will.

Jesus Responds to Mary and Joseph

Next, let's take a look at Christ's first recorded words. His parents were anxious when they realized that He had not returned from the temple with them to Nazareth. When they found Him three days later "sitting in the midst of the teachers, both listening to them and asking them questions, they were astonished," and His mother reproved Him.

> Why have You treated us this way? Behold, Your father and I have been anxiously looking for You. (Luke 2:48)

Notice the "why" question (which often is used by manipulative people to imply guilt). Notice the sympathetic appeal ("You have hurt us by making us anxious"). Perhaps you've never considered Mary's response to Jesus' behavior to be manipulative. But whether she did so consciously or unconsciously, to the extent that she tried to make Him feel guilty or responsible for her anxiety, technically, she was using manipulation.

As you read Christ's reply, see if you can pick out the two aforementioned antimanipulation devices.

> Why is it that you were looking for Me? Did *you* not know that I *had to be* in My Father's house? (Luke 2:49)

Did you catch them?

First, Jesus appealed to personal responsibility. "Did *you* not know . . . ?" Mary and Joseph, of all people, should have known (it was their responsibility to know) that Jesus was the Christ and that God had given Him certain responsibilities that He had to fulfill.

Second, Jesus made an appeal to God's will. "Did you not know *that I had to be* . . . ?" Mary and Joseph should have known that Jesus had to be seeing to the affairs of His heavenly Father, not only because of the many Old Testament prophecies written about the ministry of the Messiah, but also because of what God's agents—Gabriel (Luke 1:26–38), Zacharias (Luke 1:68–79), Simeon (Luke 2:21–35), and Anna the prophetess (Luke 2:36–38)—said concerning Him.

Jesus Responds to the Pharisees

Jesus used these antimanipulation devices in another instance when He was accused of working on the Sabbath:

> Now it happened that He was passing through some grain-fields on a Sabbath; and His disciples were picking the heads of grain, rubbing them in their hands, and eating the grain. (Luke 6:1)

On this occasion, the disciples were following Christ through some fields of standing grain. As they were walking, some of the disciples began to strip off some of the grain heads into their hands. At this point, in order to remove the outer bran shell from the inner heart of each grain, they had to first rub the kernels between their hands and then blow just hard enough to scatter the light bran covering into the air and away from the heavier heart of the kernel. In the eyes of the Pharisees, who held to their traditions more tenaciously than they did to the Bible, this "harvesting" was work and consequently unlawful to do on the Sabbath (see Ex. 34:21).

> But some of the Pharisees said, "Why do you do what is not lawful on the Sabbath?" (Luke 6:2)

Did you observe once again the "why" question? In asking this question, Jesus' accusers were likely trying to discredit (embarrass) Him, or perhaps even attempting to afflict His conscience with guilt. Regardless of their motives, the Pharisees were being manipulative, and Christ wisely detected and responded to their manipulation.

He replied, "Have *you* not even read" (notice the appeal to personal responsibility: they were Pharisees and should have known the Scriptures) "what David did when he was hungry, he and those who were with him, how he entered the house of God, and took and ate the consecrated bread which is not lawful for any to eat except the priests alone, and gave it to his companions?" (Notice the appeal to God's Word: Jesus referred them to what was recorded in 1 Samuel 21:1–6 as an exception to the law that prohibited anyone but the priests from eating the holy bread of the temple as explained in Leviticus 24:5–9). He compared Himself and His disciples to David and his men. In other words Jesus said, "If it was lawful for David and his men to break the law by eating the showbread, it is lawful for Me and My disciples to violate man-made traditions because

I am greater than David. I am the Son of Man, and the 'Son of Man is Lord of the Sabbath.' "

Jesus Responds to the Chief Priests and Scribes

After telling the parable of the vineyard owner—which was aimed at convicting some of the chief priests and scribes of their rejection of Him as the Messiah—Christ became their target. Notice their clear intent to catch Him.

> The scribes and the chief priests tried to lay hands on Him that very hour, and they feared the people; for they understood that He spoke this parable against them. So they watched Him, and sent spies who pretended to be righteous, in order that they might catch Him in some statement, so that they could deliver Him to the rule and the authority of the governor. They questioned Him, saying, "Teacher, we know that You speak and teach correctly, and You are not partial to any, but teach the way of God in truth. Is it lawful for us to pay taxes to Caesar, or not?" (Luke 20:19–22)

Notice also their flattery ("You speak and teach correctly, and You are not partial to any, but teach the way of God in truth"), which was no doubt intended to make them look sincere in front of the people. Again, they use a question ("Is it lawful . . . ?"), and not just any old question but one that attempts to limit His choices to only two options, "yes" or "no." By doing so they were hoping to set Him up to be disreputable either in the eyes of the people or in the eyes of the government.

> But He detected their trickery and said to them, "Show Me a denarius. Whose likeness and inscription does it have?" They said, "Caesar's." And He said to them, "Then [you] render to Caesar the things that are Caesar's, and to *God* the things that

are God's." And they were unable to catch Him in a saying in the presence of the people; and marveling at His answer, they became silent. (Luke 20:23–26)

Could you pick out the two devices?

First, the Lord appealed to personal responsibility—(*please note the imperative*) "*You [must] render.*" It was their responsibility to obey Caesar and pay taxes, as it was their responsibility to honor God with the first portion of their increase.

Second, He appealed to God's will—they were to give God that which the Scripture says rightfully belonged to Him. "[Render] to God the things that are God's." The word *render* means to give or do something necessary in fulfillment of an obligation or expectation.[4]

Now it's your turn to discover the antimanipulation device. Read the following account. On the lines below, explain in your own words how Jesus put a stop to the manipulation.

Jesus Responds to the Pharisees and Scribes

Then some Pharisees and scribes came to Jesus from Jerusalem and said, "Why do Your disciples break the tradition of the elders? For they do not wash their hands when they eat bread." And He answered and said to them, "And why do you yourselves transgress *the commandment of God* for the sake of your tradition? For *God said*, 'Honor your father and mother,' and, 'He who speaks evil of father or mother is to be put to death.' But you say, 'Whoever says to his father or mother, "Whatever I have that would help you has been given to God," he is not to honor his father or his mother.' And by this you invalidated the *word of God* for the sake of your tradition. You hypocrites, rightly did *Isaiah* prophesy of you:

4. Spiros Zodhiates, *The Complete Word Study Dictionary*, rev. ed. (Chattanooga, TN: AMG Publishers, 1993), 222.

'This people honors Me with their lips,
But their heart is far away from Me.
But in vain do they worship Me,
Teaching as doctrines the precepts of men.' "
(Matt. 15:1–9)

How were the Pharisees and scribes attempting to manipulate Christ? _____

_____

_____

_____

How did Jesus appeal to their personal responsibilities? _____

_____

_____

_____

_____

How did Jesus appeal to God's Word or will? _____

_____

_____

_____

_____

Jesus Responds to Mrs. Zebedee

Here is the account of how Jesus handled Mrs. Zebedee's request that her two sons sit on either side of His throne in the kingdom. See if you can find the antimanipulation techniques—this without the aid of italics.

Then the mother of the sons of Zebedee came to Jesus with her sons, bowing down and making a request of Him. And He said to her, "What do you wish?" She said to Him, "Command that in Your kingdom these two sons of mine may sit one on Your right and one on Your left." But Jesus answered, "You do not know what you are asking. Are you able to drink the cup that I am about to drink?" They said to Him, "We are able." He said to them, "My cup you shall drink; but to sit on My right and on My left, this is not Mine to give, but it is for those for whom it has been prepared by My Father." (Matt. 20:20–23)

How did Mrs. Zebedee attempt to manipulate Christ?

_____

_____

_____

_____

How did Jesus appeal to personal responsibility?

_____

_____

_____

_____

How did Jesus appeal to God's Word or will?

_____

_____

_____

_____

Search the Scriptures for yourself and you will find other examples not only of how Christ used these tools, but of other biblical characters who utilized them as well.

Detecting the Misuse of Guilt

As we have seen, the favorite tactic of those who tried to manipulate Christ was attempting to convict Him of sin that He *did not commit.* The favorite and perhaps the most effective means of manipulating others is to try to make them feel guilty.

One particular form of manipulation by the misuse of guilt is making obligatory statements. When a manipulative person (who is not your authority and therefore has no biblical basis for obligating you to do things apart from Scripture) begins a sentence with one of the following phrases, ask yourself, "Where is it written that I am obligated to do that?" Since there is no biblical mandate for you to do what you are being made to feel guilty for not doing, the manipulator is probably (consciously or otherwise) reaching for a handle to control you.

- You should
- You shouldn't
- You must
- You mustn't
- You've got to
- You'd better
- You can't
- You're supposed to
- You ought to
- You have to

Manipulative Snapshots

Let's take a look at a few scenarios to see how what we have learned about preventing manipulation can be put into practice. The applications in the "snapshots" that follow are not the only or necessarily the best utilization of these principles. Remember, there is usually more than one way to skin a cat (or ice a cake) biblically. Context and the individual personalities of both parties will greatly influence the exact wording of every answer. As you read each response, see if you can pick out both of the antimanipulation devices employed by the manipulatee.

Friend to Friend

Manipulative comment: "How can you do this to me?"

Biblical response: "Have I sinned against you? Are you upset with me about something that God isn't?"

Mother to Daughter

Manipulative comment: "I don't appreciate what you're doing to my grandchildren."

Biblical response: "God hasn't given you the responsibility to raise our children. According to the Bible, when I got married, I left your authority and established a new decision-making unit with my spouse. It is wrong for you to not let us leave and cleave by imposing on us your unbiblical standards. We certainly welcome any biblical input and support you can provide in reference to our parenting, but the final decision about how we raise our children is ours, not yours."

Husband to Wife

Manipulative comment: "How could you possibly talk to me about my sin when yours is so much worse than mine?"

Biblical response: "Sweetheart, it is your responsibility to convict me of my sin as it is my responsibility to convict you of yours. The Bible says that when you reprove me I should heed your reproof, and when I reprove you, you should heed mine. I will be more than happy to respond biblically to your concerns about my sin after we finish talking about yours."

Employer to Employee

Manipulative comment: "If you were a team player, you wouldn't mind putting in extra time on the weekend."

Biblical response: "I am a Christian and have to play by God's rules. God says I must serve my employer with sincerity and honesty, but He also has given me other responsibilities outside of this job, which I cannot neglect. I can't always work the weekends without sinning against my Lord. Do you think it is right for an employer to ask his employee to violate his religious convictions?"

Husband to Wife

Manipulative comment: "If you really loved me, you would cover for me."

Biblical response: "Love doesn't rejoice in iniquity but rejoices in the truth. It is because I love you that I cannot lie for you."

Wife to Husband

Manipulative comment: "That's just like you men. You're all so selfish."

Biblical response: "My Bible teaches that all women are sinners and therefore just as selfish as men."

Church Leader to Church Member

Manipulative comment: "If your priorities were right, you'd be here (at church) every time the doors were opened."

Biblical response: "Brother, where exactly does it say in the Bible that Christians are supposed to be at church every time the doors are opened? Haven't you taught us that God has given Christians other priorities besides their ecclesiastical responsibilities?"

Sharpening Your Skills

To effectively deal with the wily ploys of the manipulator, you will need to become proficient in your ability to apply what you have learned in this booklet. You will have to practice implementing Proverbs 26:4–5. You will need to become at least as good at preventing manipulation as your foil is at attempting it.

The "Manipulation Worksheet" that follows is a tool to help you "ponder" how to answer those who routinely manipulate you *and* to train yourself how to "answer a fool as his folly deserves."

> The heart of the righteous ponders how to answer,
> But the mouth of the wicked pours out evil things.
> (Prov. 15:28)

Appendix: Manipulation Worksheet

Circumstances surrounding manipulation:

_____

_____

_____

_____

_____

Manipulative remarks made to me:

_____

_____

_____

_____

_____

My response to the manipulation:

_____

_____

_____

_____

_____

Christlike/biblical response to the manipulation:

_____

_____

_____

_____

_____

Circumstances Surrounding Manipulation

By recording the circumstances that surround the manipulation, you can ensure that an attempt to sinfully control is examined in its proper context. This will also better enable you to detect any "common denominators" or patterns of what triggers repeated attempts at manipulation, as well as the situations in which those attempts are made.

Your purpose in filling in this worksheet is to examine each conflict as though you were looking at a videotape of a boxing match after losing the fight. You will watch it at least two times: first, to observe the style, technique, and strategy of your opponent so that you can learn how to prevail against him in the future; second, to look for your mistakes in order to plan ahead for the next confrontation.

Manipulative Remarks Made to Me

Recording verbatim (or as accurately as possible) the words chosen by the tactician will help break down cunning subterfuge into its component parts. As each manipulative remark is examined, look for the following:

- The exact form of manipulative behavior (accusations, "why" questions, obligatory statements, etc.)
- The possible desired emotional response (guilt, shame, fear, etc.)
- The possible desired controlling effect (procrastination, lowering of standards, etc.)
- The possible sinful motives (love of pleasure, power, praise, etc.)

At this point, I must raise two notes of warning. First, we may judge actions and words, but we may not lawfully judge the thoughts and motives of another without confirmation.

Therefore do not go on passing judgment before the time, *but wait until the Lord comes who will* both bring to light the things hidden in the darkness and *disclose the motives of men's hearts*; and then each man's praise will come to him from God. (1 Cor. 4:5; see also 1 Sam. 16:7; Luke 16:15)

As previously mentioned, the reason for examining "possible" internal areas is for *possible* use later on in helping the manipulator examine his own heart (i.e., "Could it be that the reason you said that was to make me feel guilty?").

Second, be sure that the remarks you perceived as manipulative truly were manipulative. In other words, you should be certain that you have enough evidence to make the "manipulation" diagnosis. To do otherwise would be to answer a matter before hearing it, and to have it become folly and shame to you (Prov. 18:13).

My Response to the Manipulation

Having confirmed that you have been manipulated, you are now going to record verbatim how you responded to the manipulator. As you consider your answer, notice how the manipulator got you off track and the bait that was used to lure you into the snare. Try to recall and identify your emotions, thoughts, and motives. Then evaluate them biblically.

Christlike/Biblical Response to the Manipulation

This is the most important part of the worksheet. It's at this point that you will reconstruct your answer to reflect the wisdom of Christ. Here is where you determine how to integrate into your response one or both of the scriptural antimanipulation techniques at which we've just looked. This will take time, but it will be "time well invested" as your level of skill and confidence will increase in direct proportion to your investment.

Study the following completed worksheet. In the space provided, see if you can come up with *another* Christlike/biblical response based on what you have learned.

Sample Manipulation Worksheet

Circumstances surrounding manipulation:

My mother-in-law, who is a professing Christian, called to inform me that the whole family was going to the beach for the holidays. She also told me that most of the extended family was coming from out of town and that everyone was looking forward to seeing how much our children had grown. The problem is, six weeks ago I told *both* of my in-laws, very deliberately, that this year we were going out of state to visit *my* family, whom I haven't seen in several years. When I tried to remind her of this, she became huffy.

1. Manipulative remarks made to me:

"But you always spend the holidays with us! Everyone will be so disappointed. I don't know what I'm going to tell them."

2. My response to the manipulation:

"Well, perhaps you can tell them that we had a miscommunication."

3. Christlike/biblical response to the manipulation:

"I'm sure the Lord would want you to tell them the truth."

My Christlike/biblical response to the manipulation:

_____
_____
_____

1. Manipulative remarks made to me:

"Well, OK. If you want to let down everyone in the family, don't come."

2. My response to the manipulation:

"It's not that I want to let anyone down; it's a matter of our making other plans."

3. Christlike/biblical response:

"I don't want to let down my Lord. He's commanded me to keep my promises and to honor my parents; shouldn't you be encouraging me to fulfill both of these biblical responsibilities?"

My Christlike/biblical response to the manipulation:

_____

_____

_____

_____

1. Manipulative remarks made to me:

"But what about us? You're supposed to honor us too."

2. My response to the manipulation:

"We have honored you every year for the last six years by spending the holidays at your beach house."

3. Christlike/biblical response:

"Mom, aren't you being selfish and ungrateful? The Bible says we should "not merely look out for our own personal interests, but also for the interests of others.""

My Christlike/biblical response to the manipulation:

_____

_____

_____

_____

I trust that you now have a better idea of the extent to which you have been manipulated—or at least a greater confidence in your ability to detect and respond to manipulative ploys others may use to selfishly control you in the future. On the pages that follow there are additional manipulation worksheets for you to utilize as you learn how to apply the wisdom of Proverbs 26:4–5 in the power of the Spirit of Jesus Christ.

> But the wisdom from above is first pure, then peaceable, gentle, reasonable, full of mercy and good fruits, unwavering, without hypocrisy. And the seed whose fruit is righteousness is sown in peace by those who make peace. (James 3:17–18)

Circumstances surrounding manipulation:

_____
_____
_____
_____

Manipulative remarks made to me:

_____
_____
_____
_____

My response to the manipulation:

_____
_____
_____
_____

Christlike/biblical response to the manipulation:

_____
_____
_____
_____

Circumstances surrounding manipulation:

_____

_____

_____

_____

_____

Manipulative remarks made to me:

_____

_____

_____

_____

_____

My response to the manipulation:

_____

_____

_____

_____

_____

Christlike/biblical response to the manipulation:

_____

_____

_____

_____

_____

Circumstances surrounding manipulation:

_____

_____

_____

_____

_____

Manipulative remarks made to me:

_____

_____

_____

_____

_____

My response to the manipulation:

_____

_____

_____

_____

_____

Christlike/biblical response to the manipulation:

_____

_____

_____

_____

_____

Circumstances surrounding manipulation:

_____

_____

_____

_____

_____

Manipulative remarks made to me:

_____

_____

_____

_____

_____

My response to the manipulation:

_____

_____

_____

_____

_____

Christlike/biblical response to the manipulation:

_____

_____

_____

_____

_____